Shadows

Louise and Richard
Spilsbury

Raintree is an imprint of Capstone Global Library Limited, a company incorporated in England and Wales having its registered office at 264 Banbury Road, Oxford OX2 7DY – Registered company number: 6695582

www.raintree.co.uk
myorders@raintree.co.uk

Edited by Penny West
Designed by Rich Parker
Picture research by Tracy Cummins
Production by Helen McCreath
Originated by Capstone Global Library Ltd
Printed and bound in China by CTPS

ISBN 978 1 406 29910 6 (hardback)
19 18 17 16 15
10 9 8 7 6 5 4 3 2 1

ISBN 978 1 406 29915 1 (paperback)
20 19 18 17 16
10 9 8 7 6 5 4 3 2 1

Spilsbury, Louise and Richard
Shadows (Exploring Light)

British Library Cataloguing in Publication Data
A full catalogue record for this book is available from the British Library.

Acknowledgements
We would like to thank the following for permission to reproduce photographs:
Capstone Press: Karon Dubke, 8, 9, 12, 13, 16, 17, 19, 20, 21, 24, 25, 28, 29; Getty Images: Andy Crawford, 5, Otto Stadler, 15, Sean Malyon, 26, Sue Flood, 11, Tony Anderson, 14; iStockphoto: Oktay Ortakcioglu, 27, werd678, 10; Science Source: GIPhotoStock, 18; Shutterstock: agsandrew, Design Element, ALMAGAMI, Design Element, ANP, 6, Click Bestsellers, Design Element, Dennis Tokarzewski, Design Element, dotshock, Cover, ID1974, Design Element, Khafizov Ivan Harisovich, 4, luckypic, Design Element, MaPaSa, 22, Michelangelus, 23, Pavel Vakhrushev, 7, Shutterstock/Vass Zoltan, Design Element.

We would like to thank Catherine Jones for her invaluable help in the preparation of this book.

Every effort has been made to contact copyright holders of material reproduced in this book. Any omissions will be rectified in subsequent printings if notice is given to the publisher.

All the Internet addresses (URLs) given in this book were valid at the time of going to press. However, due to the dynamic nature of the Internet, some addresses may have changed, or sites may have changed or ceased to exist since publication. While the author and publisher regret any inconvenience this may cause readers, no responsibility for any such changes can be accepted by either the author or the publisher.

Contents

Some words are shown in bold, **like this**. You can find out what they mean by looking in the glossary.

Shadows

When do you notice your shadow? Have you seen it outside on a sunny day or inside when you stand in the light from a lamp? All sorts of **solid** objects can make shadows. Trees, swings, animals, buildings, cars and other things can all make shadows. Shadows can move with us when we move, too. Have you ever tried to chase your shadow? What happens when you wave to your shadow?

Many things can make shadows outdoors when the Sun is shining.

When light cannot pass through an object, the place where the light cannot reach is called a shadow.

A shadow is the dark shape an object makes when it blocks light. The shadow takes on the shape of the object that makes the shadow. A shadow can be cast when light is blocked from any **light source** such as a candle, a torch, a lamp or the Sun. When an object blocks light, a shadow appears in the area behind the object.

Shadow seeking

Take a look around and see what other things have shadows, too. How many did you find?

Making shadows

Shadows happen because light moves in straight lines called **rays**. Rays of light from a **light source** keep travelling in a straight line until they hit something else. When light hits a **solid** object like a tree, the tree **absorbs** a lot of the light. Because the tree soaks up a lot of the light that hits it, the area behind the tree where the light would have gone appears dark. It forms a shadow in the shape of the tree.

Light travels in straight lines. When light hits an object that it cannot pass through, a shadow is formed.

Shadows are not totally black because some light is reflected from the surfaces around them into the area of the shadow.

Shadows do not look totally dark or black. That is because some light is **reflected** from the area around the tree and lands in the shadow. When light reflects, it bounces off something. When light hits the ground around the tree, some of it reflects into the shadow area and stops it being so dark.

Light up our world

When light hits an object, it is reflected (bounces off) and enters our eyes. This is how we see the object.

Activity: Light lines

Test if light really does travel in straight lines.

What you need
- a ruler
- four pieces of card
- a pencil
- a straw
- Blutac or modelling clay
- books
- a torch.

What to do

1 Use your ruler to draw two diagonal lines from corner to corner across three of the four cards to make an X. Now use the sharp end of the pencil to make a hole exactly where the X meets in the middle. Wiggle the pencil to make the holes big enough for the straw to go through.

2 Use the straw to line up the three holes on the cards. Then use blobs of Blutac to hold the cards in position with the holes lined up. Remove the straw. Use Blutac to stand the fourth card behind the last card. Pile up some books until the torch is at a height where it can shine through the hole in the first card. What happens?

fourth card

second card

3 Now move the second card in the row and reattach it to the table so that it does not line up with the others. Shine a torch through the hole in the first card. What happens?

What happens?

Light usually travels in straight lines called **rays** from **light sources**. When the three holes on the cards are lined up, the light can travel through the holes and should hit the exact middle of the final card, too. When you move the middle card to one side so that the holes are not lined up, the light cannot pass through to the end. The card blocks its path and stops it moving further.

What blocks light?

Materials that block light are called **opaque**. Opaque materials are things like wood, metal or stone that stop light passing through them. That is why opaque objects make dark shadows. **Translucent** things, such as tissue paper and net curtains, make faint shadows. Translucent materials let some light through, but they **scatter** the light in all directions. You can see through them, but not clearly. You cannot see through opaque materials at all.

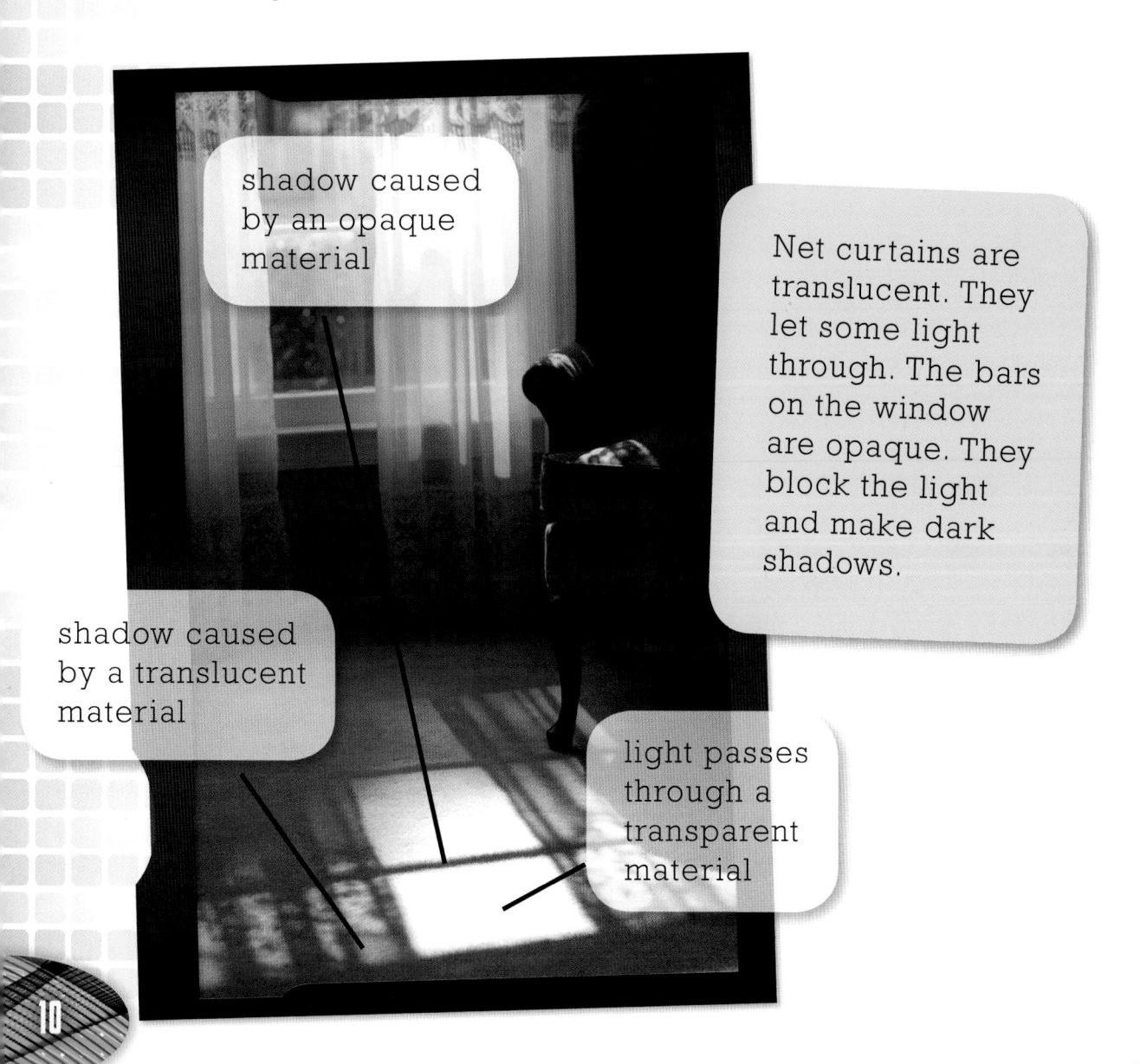

shadow caused by an opaque material

Net curtains are translucent. They let some light through. The bars on the window are opaque. They block the light and make dark shadows.

shadow caused by a translucent material

light passes through a transparent material

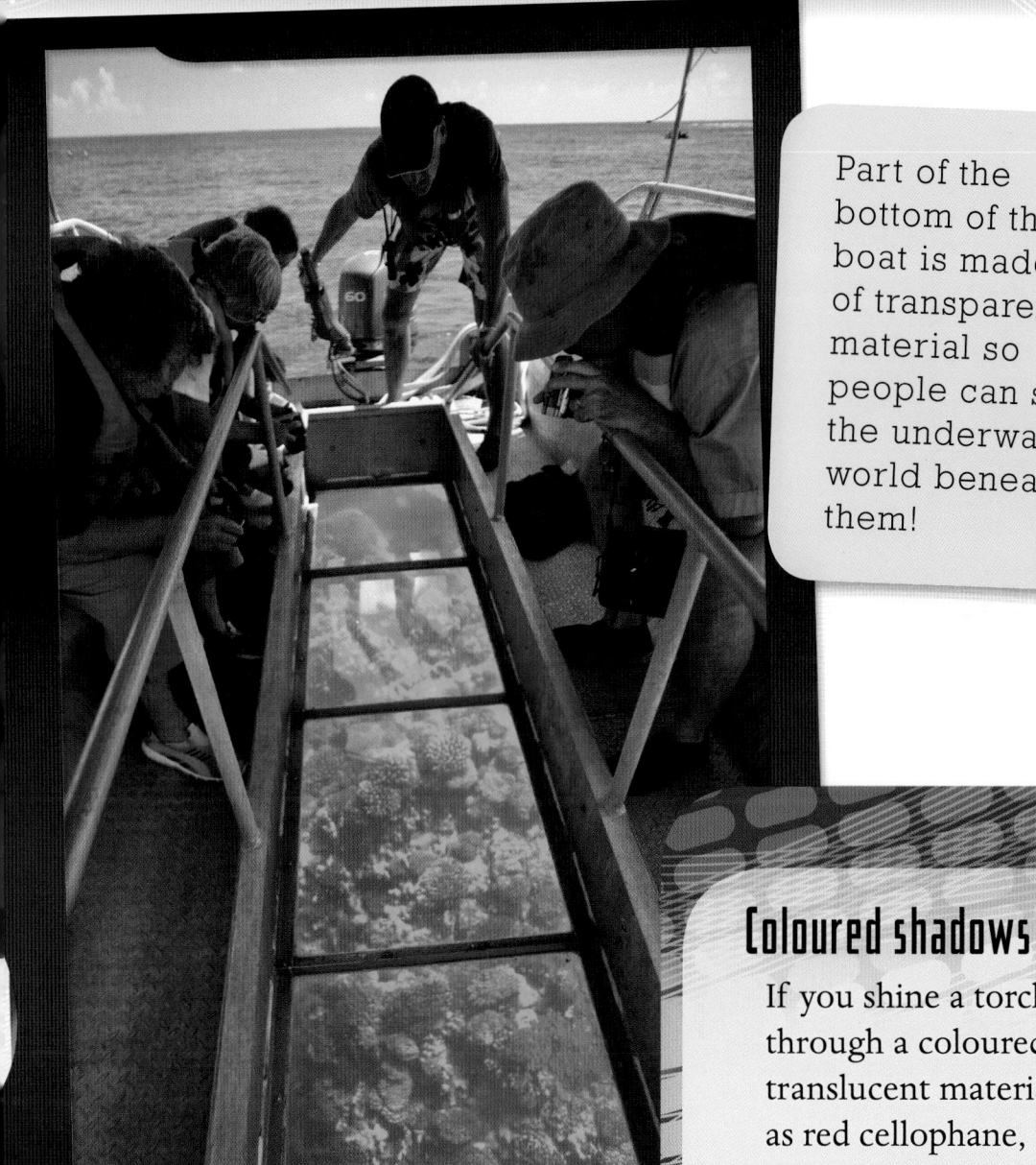

Part of the bottom of this boat is made of transparent material so people can see the underwater world beneath them!

Coloured shadows

If you shine a torch through a coloured translucent material, such as red cellophane, tissue paper or a coloured glass, you can make a coloured shadow. Try it for yourself!

Some objects and materials do not make any shadows because they do not block light at all. **Transparent** materials let light pass straight through them easily. Water, clear plastic and glass are all transparent. You can't make shadows with transparent objects, but they are useful. Windows are made from transparent glass so they let light in and we can see outside.

Activity: Light testers

Test some **materials** to find out if they are **opaque**, **translucent** or **transparent**.

What you need

- scissors
- three kitchen roll tubes
- ruler
- six different materials, such as tissue paper, greaseproof paper, clingfilm, aluminium foil, card, bubble wrap
- six elastic bands.

What to do

1 Cut each of the three kitchen rolls in half so you have six tubes. Then cut out 15-centimetre (6-inch) squares of each one of the different test materials. It is important they are the same size so this is a fair test.

2 Wrap one square of material round one end of each tube. Hold each piece of material in place using an elastic band. Make sure the material is stretched over the end and held in place tightly.

3 Hold each tube up into the light, one at a time. (Do not point your tube directly at the Sun or a very bright light as this could hurt your eye.) Look through the open end of each tube. How much light gets through each one?

What happens?

When you look through the different materials you should be able to divide them into three groups: opaque, translucent and transparent. If the material is transparent, like the clingfilm, light passes through it easily. If the object is translucent, like the tissue paper, it will let some light through but not clearly. If the object is opaque, like the foil, it blocks light completely.

Shadow shapes

We can often guess what something is by the shadow it makes, but not always. If the **light source** is directly behind an object, its shadow is similar in shape to that object. Shadow shapes change when the edge of the object facing the light source changes. That is why the shape of your shadow changes if you are facing towards a light source and then turn to the side. That is also why objects of different shapes can make similar shadow shapes.

When shadows combine, they can make different shapes so that we cannot tell what made them!

One puppeteer works all the puppets in an Indonesian shadow puppet show and a show can last all night!

Shadow puppets are some of the oldest types of puppets in the world. The puppets are flat and cut from leather or another **opaque material**. A puppeteer moves the puppets in front of a lamp to create shadows that the audience sees through a **translucent** screen.

Indonesian shadow puppets

The most famous shadow puppets come from Java, an island in Indonesia. They have been used to tell stories for over 1000 years. The puppets are cut from buffalo skin and decorated with paint. Tiny holes all over the puppet create the outlines and textures of the characters' clothes.

Activity: Shadow puppets

You can use your hands to make your own shadow puppets.

What you need

- a torch
- a dark room
- hands!

What to do

1 Turn on the torch in a dark room and rest it on a table so that it points at a blank wall. Move your hands in front of the light to find out where is the best place to make shadows on the wall.

2 Use your hands to make shadows. To make a dog, hold your hand out flat, palm facing to the side, fold back your index finger and hold your little finger away from the other two middle fingers.

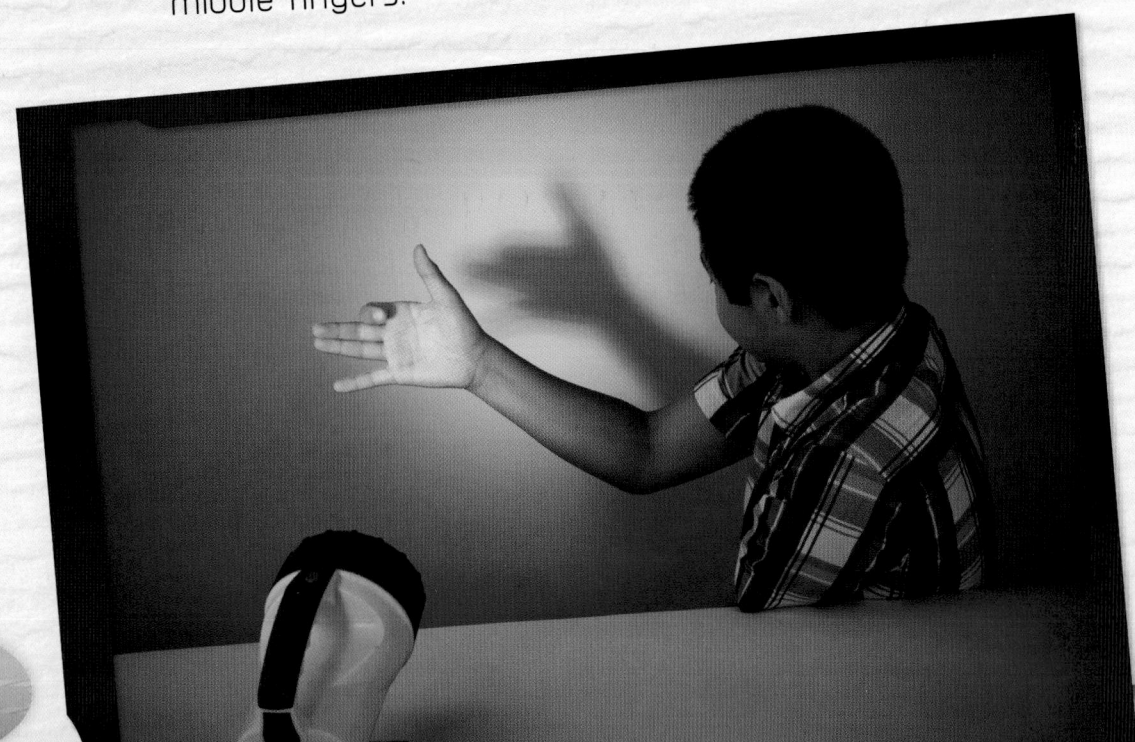

3 To make a bird or bat, link your two thumbs together and spread out your hands to form wings. You can "flap" your hands to make it look like your animal is flying!

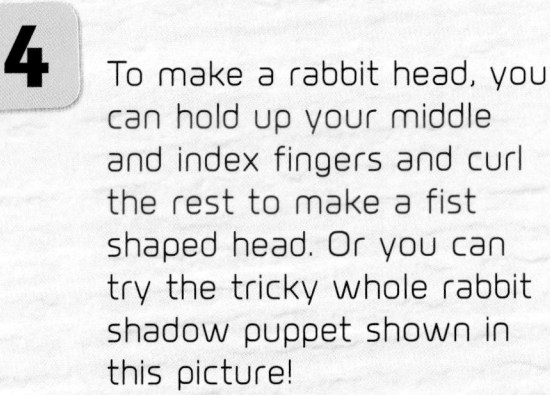

4 To make a rabbit head, you can hold up your middle and index fingers and curl the rest to make a fist shaped head. Or you can try the tricky whole rabbit shadow puppet shown in this picture!

What happens?

Your hands only show the shape in **silhouette** so you can create all sorts of shapes with your hands that look like characters. You can find more ideas in books and on the Internet or play around to create your own. When you have learned how to do these well, maybe you could write a story and put on a puppet show?

Shadow sizes

Shadows come in many different sizes. A small object usually makes a small shadow and a large object usually makes a large shadow. Shadows can get bigger or smaller depending on how far away they are from a **light source**. When an object is far away from a light source, it casts a shadow that is about the same size as that object. When you move an object closer to a light source, the shadow looks bigger than the object itself.

The chess piece closer to the light source makes the bigger shadow.

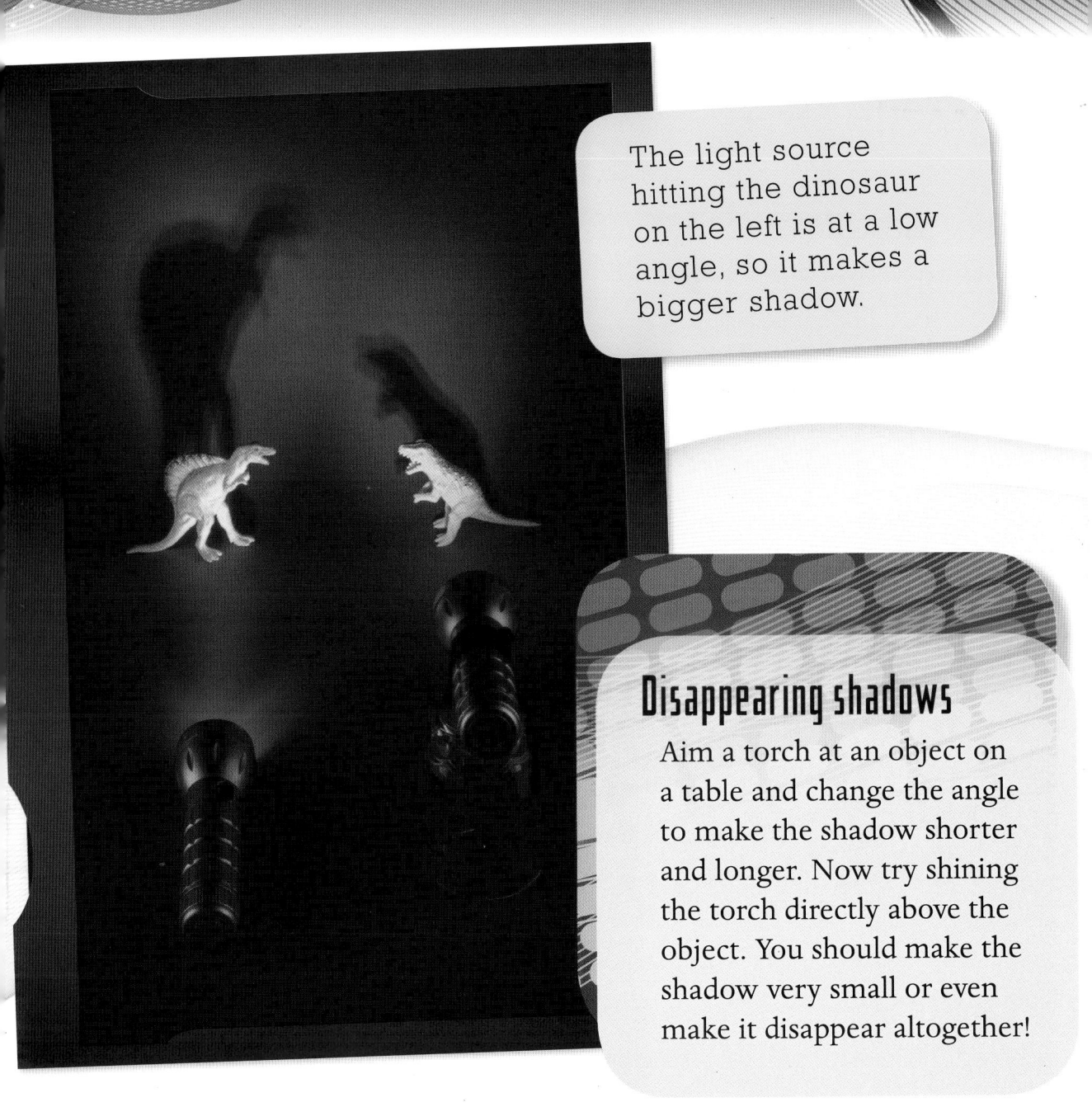

The light source hitting the dinosaur on the left is at a low angle, so it makes a bigger shadow.

Disappearing shadows

Aim a torch at an object on a table and change the angle to make the shadow shorter and longer. Now try shining the torch directly above the object. You should make the shadow very small or even make it disappear altogether!

Shadows can also get longer or shorter. The length of a shadow depends on the position or **angle** of the light source that hits the object. If the light comes from a high or steep angle above the object, less light is blocked and the shadow is short. When the light source is low and aimed at the side of an object, the shadow is longer because the object blocks more light.

Activity: Silhouettes

Make **silhouettes** of your friends and family to hang on the wall.

What to do

1 Put the chair and your model sitting sideways in front of a wall.

2 Position the lamp so the light is shining straight at the side of your model's face. You need to see the shadow of their **profile** on the wall. Change the distance between the lamp and your model until the shadow is clear. What happens to the size of the shadow when they are closer to the lamp?

What you need

- a chair
- a friend or parent to be your model
- an adjustable lamp
- a large sheet of coloured paper
- a pencil
- scissors
- glue
- a large sheet of white paper.

3 Tape the coloured paper onto the wall, so it covers the shadow of your model's head. Ask the model to keep very still while you use the pencil to carefully trace around the outline of their head. (Do not get in between the model and the light or you will not be able to see the shadow.)

4 Cut the shape out. This is a silhouette of your model! If you like, you can glue the silhouette to a sheet of white paper, to make it stand out even more.

What happens?

You can change the size of the shadow to make bigger and smaller silhouettes, but you also want them to have a clear outline or edge. When the model is closer to the light, more light is blocked out, so the shadow is bigger. If the model is further from the light, less light is blocked out, so the shadow is smaller. But it will get sharper as the object moves further from the light and fuzzier as the object moves closer to the light.

Objects close to a **light source** block a lot of light, so they make big, fuzzy shadows. Objects further from a light source block a little light, so they make small, clear shadows.

Changing shadows

Have you ever noticed that shadows outside are longer in the morning and afternoon than they are at midday? This is because the position of the Sun in the sky changes during the day. When the Sun is low in the sky at the beginning and end of the day, shadows are longer. In the middle of the day, the Sun is directly above us and casts the shortest shadows. Shadows change as the **angle** of light **rays** from the Sun changes.

Next time it is a sunny day, go outside and look at your own shadow. Try it in the early morning or later afternoon and at midday. What is the difference?

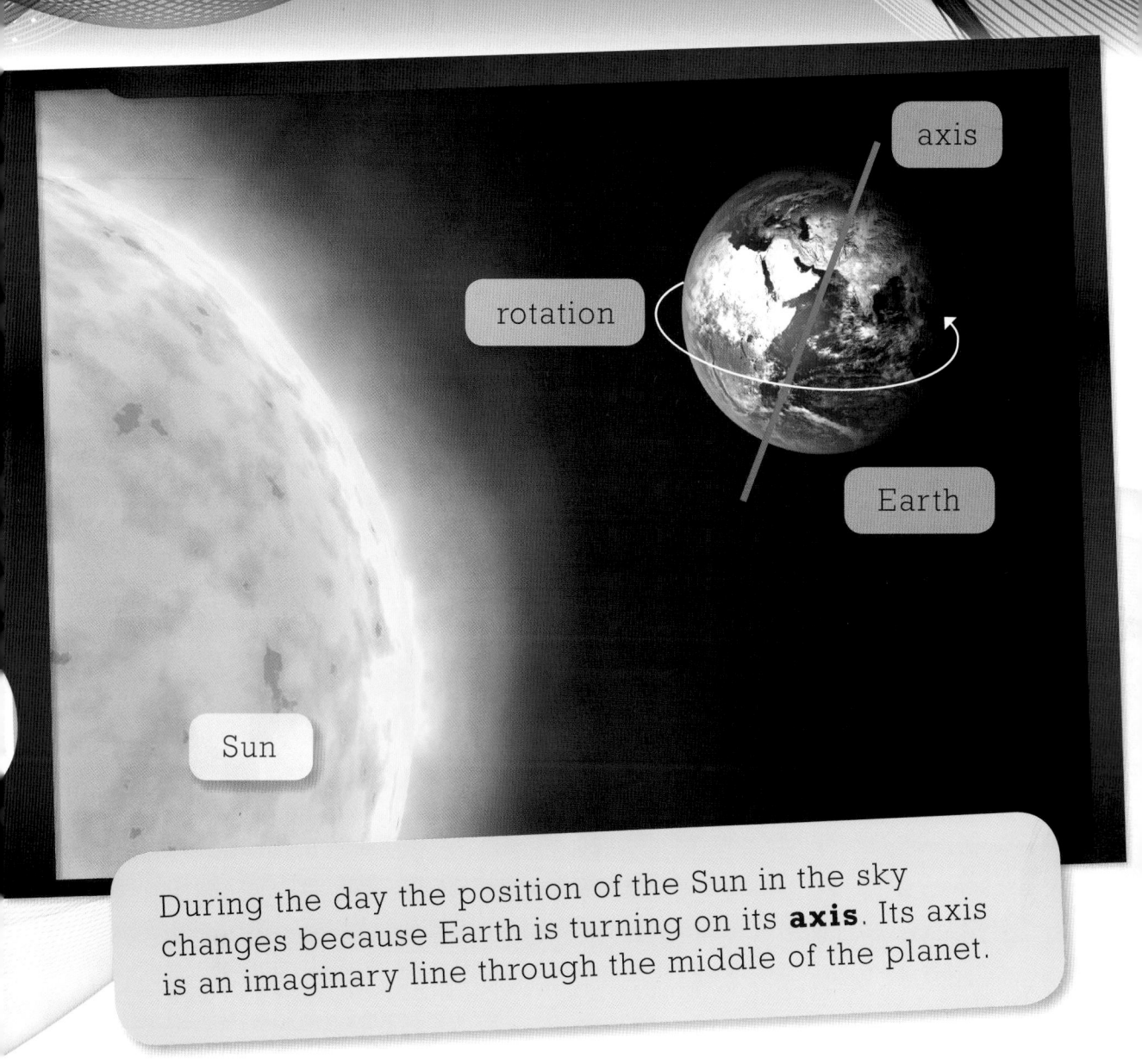

axis

rotation

Earth

Sun

During the day the position of the Sun in the sky changes because Earth is turning on its **axis**. Its axis is an imaginary line through the middle of the planet.

The Sun appears to move around the Earth, but this is not what is happening. It is Earth that is moving. Earth is like a big ball that is spinning slowly all the time. When Earth rotates, the angle at which the Sun's light strikes you changes. That is why shadows change length during the day. Earth spins in the same direction all the time, so shadows always move in the same direction, too.

Activity: Sundial

Make a sundial that you can use to tell the time. Start this activity in the morning on a sunny day when you will be home all day.

What you need

- a sharp pencil
- a large paper cup with a plastic lid and a straw
- some stones or sand
- sticky tape
- a compass
- chalk
- a watch
- a pen.

What to do

1 Use the pencil to make a hole in the side of the cup about 5 centimetres (2 inches) down from the top.

2 Put the stones or sand in the bottom of the cup and then put the lid on the cup. Push the straw through the hole on the lid and the hole in the side. Leave about 5 centimetres (2 inches) sticking out of the top of the cup. Secure the straw to the cup by taping it down on the side.

3 Find a spot outside where the Sun shines for most of the day and put the sundial on a flat surface. Use your compass to stand the cup so the straw points towards north. Mark the position of the base of the cup with chalk, so that you can put it back in exactly the same spot again another day.

4 Use your watch to mark where the straw's shadow falls on the cup at 10.00 a.m. Draw a short line on the lid and write the number 10. Repeat this on the hour, every hour until the Sun goes down.

5 Put your sundial back in the same position on the next sunny day and check it works. Compare the times on the sundial to the time on your watch.

What happens?

You should notice that the shadow is in different positions at different times of the day and that it changes length. The sundial works by casting a shadow in different positions, at different times of the day. Long ago people used sundials to tell the time during daylight hours.

In the shade

Shadows can be useful. On a sunny day it is a good idea to sit in the **shade**. Shade is the darkness made by a shadow when you are outside. When you sit in the shade created by the shadow of a tree, less sunlight hits your skin. The Sun can burn your skin. In summer you can also wear a hat and long-sleeved shirt made from **opaque materials** to block sunlight and stop it from reaching your skin.

On a hot day, it is good to find shade made by the shadow of something big like a tree.

It is important to wear sunglasses on mountains. Sunlight reflecting off the snow makes it hard to see and can hurt your eyes.

Shadows also help us to keep cool. It is cooler in a shadow because the area is blocked from the Sun's light. When sunlight reaches and heats the ground, the warmth **reflects** and heats the air above the surface, too. That is why a shadow from an umbrella or a big hat helps to keep you cool.

Sun safety

Translucent sunglasses protect your eyes from sun damage but allow you to see on sunny days. You should never look directly at the Sun, even when you are wearing sunglasses. It could cause permanent eye damage.

Activity: Snow goggles

Before sunglasses were invented, Inuit people in the Arctic made special goggles to protect their eyes from the glare of the Sun off the snow. They often made theirs from reindeer antlers or bone. You can make some from card.

What to do

1 Cut a piece of thin, bendy card into a rectangle about 15 centimetres (6 inches) long and 10 centimetres (4 inches) wide.

2 Hold the card over your eyes and make a mark where your nose touches it. Cut out a bridge for your nose from the bottom centre of the card so it can sit closer to your face.

3 Use a ruler to draw a line across the middle of the card on either side of the nose bridge. Ask an adult to help you cut two long, thin slits in the card, no more than about 1 centimetre (a quarter of an inch) wide.

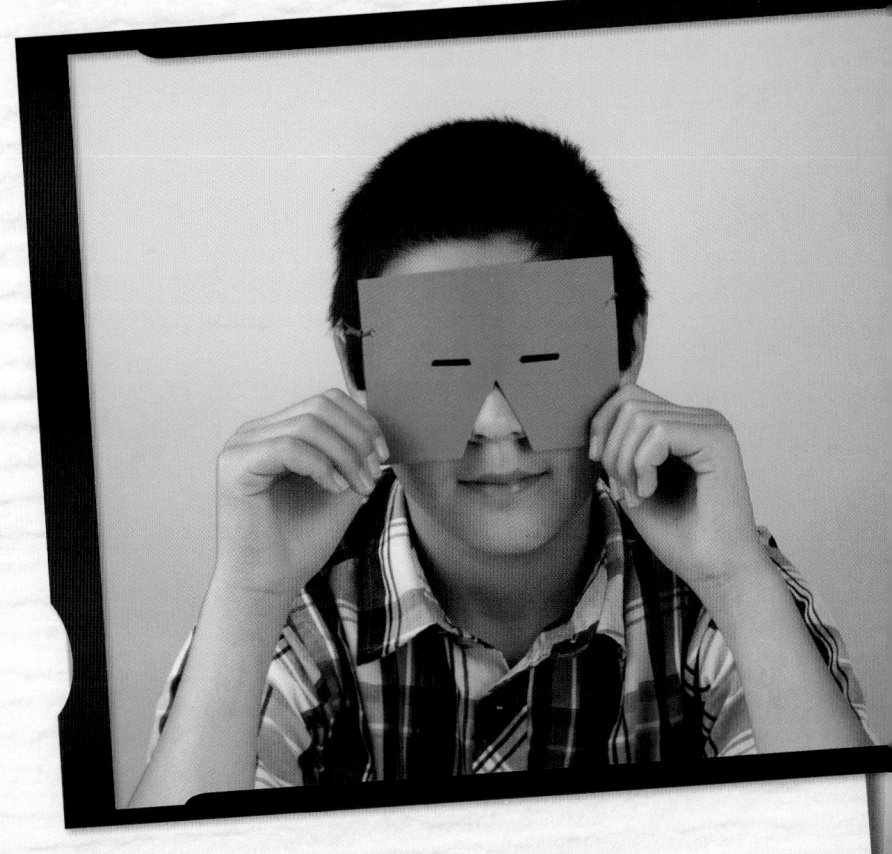

4 Use the sharp pencil to make two holes, one in each of the top corners of the goggles. Tie a piece of string about 30 centimetres (12 inches) long to each hole. Put the goggles over your eyes and tie the string behind your head.

5 Go outside into the daylight. How do you think the snow goggles work?

What happens?

The snow goggles fit tightly against the face to block light from above, below and the sides. The only light enters from the narrow slits in the front. This **shades** the eyes from most of the Sun's light.

Glossary

absorb to soak up or take in something. A sponge absorbs water.

angle amount or measure of a turn between two straight lines that meet at one end

axis imaginary line through the middle of Earth, between the North and South Poles

light source something that makes or gives off light, such as the Sun or a torch

material something we use or make other things from, such as wood, rubber or plastic

opaque something you cannot see through

profile outline of something, usually a person's face

ray narrow line or beam of light

reflect to bounce back light off a surface

scatter to reflect light in all directions

shade darkness made by a shadow when you are outside

silhouette dark shape and outline of someone or something set against a lighter background

solid thing that has a definite shape and always takes up the same amount of space. Many solids are hard, such as wood or metal.

translucent something that lets some but not all light through

transparent something you can see through

Find out more

Books

Why Does Light Cast Shadows? (Investigating Science), Jacqui Bailey (Wayland, 2010)

The Cave of Shadows - Explore Light and Use Science to Survive (Science Adventures), Louise & Richard Spilsbury (Franklin Watts, 2013)

Shadows and Reflections (Light All Around Us), Daniel Nunn (Raintree, 2012)

What are Shadows and Reflections? (Light & Sound Waves Close-Up), Robin Johnson (Crabtree Publishing, 2014)

Websites

etc.usf.edu/clipart/galleries/266-hand-shadow-puppetry

On this website there are 15 examples of hand shadow puppets to make.

www.bbc.co.uk/schools/scienceclips/ages/7_8/light_shadows.shtml

You can experiment with light and shadows on this interactive site.

www.childrensuniversity.manchester.ac.uk/interactives/science/earthandbeyond/shadows

Visit this University of Manchester website to learn more about how the Sun creates shadows on Earth.

www.nasa.gov/audience/forstudents/k-4/stories/F_Keeping_Cool_With_Shadows.html

Find out more about shadows and shadows in space on this NASA website.

Index